Tales of Heaven and Earth

Bernard Merdrignac lives by the sea,
just across the water from the British Isles.
He teaches medieval history at Rennes in Brittany
and is particularly interested in the lives of Celtic saints.

Cover design by Peter Bennett

Bible quotations are taken from
The New English Bible (1970).

ISBN: 1 85103 256 8
© Editions Gallimard, 1994
Managing editor: Jacqueline Vallon
Adviser for UK edition: Rev. David Jarmy
English text © 1996 by Moonlight Publishing Ltd
First published in the United Kingdom 1997
by Moonlight Publishing Ltd, 36 Stratford Road, London W8
Printed in Italy by Editoriale Zanardi

WHEN BRENDAN DISCOVERED PARADISE

by Bernard Merdrignac

Illustrated by Nicolas Wintz

Translated by Gwen Marsh

Moonlight Publishing

*For Aine and Liam
who have often been
in my thoughts
as I wrote this story*

Brendan chose the life of a monk rather than that of a king in Ireland.

Brendan is said to have been the Abbot of Ardfert (the hill of the tombs, in Irish), in Munster. He founded other religious houses, among them Clonfert (from the Irish cluain, a meadow). Like Saint Giles in-the-Fields in London, the name is a reminder of the rural character of the monasteries.

Brendan was not a nobody. He was high born and could have been a king in Ireland. But declining a throne, he became a monk and, against his will, found himself head of an abbey of three thousand brothers who looked up to him as their leader and holy father. He loved to go alone in the dusk of evening to the top of the cliffs near his monastery. There he would rest and watch the red disc of the sun as it went down into the empty ocean beyond which there was no-one, no-one at all.

He had heard stories about holy monks who had ventured

"The empty ocean beyond which there is no-one" is an expression borrowed from Saint Patrick (5th century). In his *Confession* he spoke thus of the western ocean seen from Ireland, where he sailed from Great Britain bringing Christianity.

westwards across the sea. It was said that they had come to magical islands where it was never too cold nor too hot and the still air was filled with sweet scents and soft melodies. Could it be that they had reached the earthly Paradise that Brendan so longed to see and constantly prayed to God to show him?

The Abbot chose fourteen of his best monks and told them of his project. So enthusiastic were they that he warned them: "We do not know what awaits us. Let us fast for three days a week for forty days that God may bring us into a safe haven." As for himself, he prayed night and day. Just as he was on the point of falling asleep exhausted, he was dazzled by a flash of coloured lightning and saw an angel standing there beside him: "Brendan, that you have kept the curiosity of a child is not something to regret. God approves of your departure. But to overcome the difficulties awaiting you and your companions, you must have great trust in him."

It was with deep emotion that Brendan quit his monastery. He left the Prior in charge. With his fourteen companions he went to the place since called Brendan's Leap, a rocky promontory that runs far out into the sea. Below, was a little sheltered creek where a narrow stream tumbled down over the rocks to the sea. Brendan had

A fast consists of going without some or all food in order to be reconciled with God. The Church suggests fasting during Lent (forty days up to Easter), Advent (the four weeks up to Christmas), the eves of holy days and each Friday.

Angels are seen as messengers between God and humans. That is why they are portrayed with wings.

According to the Bible God placed Adam and Eve in a beautiful place called the Garden of Eden. After their disobedience they were driven out of this paradise (a word from the Greek paradeisos, garden) and angels stand guard forever at the gates.

Above, the *Garden of Delights*, after Hieronymus Bosch (16th century).

The prior governs the monks under the direction of the abbot, whom he will one day succeed.

A curragh is a light vessel used in Celtic countries. It consists of a wooden framework over which animal skins are stretched. It is something like the Inuit's kayak.

arranged for the materials for building a curragh to be brought to this spot. He seemed to have grown twenty years younger: he was everywhere, eager and impatient, giving orders here, joining in the work there. His monks were busy making a framework of ash wood which they covered with cowhide. Then they caulked the ship with grease so that it would sail swiftly through the water. Brendan had all the necessary rigging and provisions for forty days stowed on board, nothing more.

Midsummer's Feast of Saint John, June 24, was fixed for the departure.

"Come aboard," Brendan cried to the brothers. "Give thanks to God: the wind is right!"

Then at the last moment, with loud shouts and much waving of arms, three monks whom Brendan had left in his abbey came running. They begged him to let them go with him. The Saint, who could see into the future, said to them: "Come on then, since you are so keen... Satan

Brendan's Leap was probably Cape Brendan on the Dingle peninsula in south-west Ireland (in red on the map on p 5), where a mountain dedicated to Saint Brendan (645 m. high) seems to dive into the sea.

The rigging means all the boat's sailing equipment.

One day his dream came true: he was to set sail in search of Paradise.

The Feast of Saint John, June 24, coincides with the summer solstice. The night was traditionally celebrated with, among other things, the lighting of bonfires.

will take two of you. As for the third, God will sustain him!"

Raising his right hand, Brendan blessed the crew. The mast was set and the sails spread. A wind from the east sprang up as by a miracle and drove them westwards. They were soon out in the open sea with nothing more in sight but sea and clouds. Although the wind filled the sails, they pulled hard on the oars, so eager were they to reach the earthly Paradise.

Satan, chief of the demons, from a detail of *The Last Judgment* by Hans Memling (15th century).

He sets sail with seventeen monks, trusting in Providence for guidance.

"Do not be afraid," which keeps recurring in this story, is a reference to the Gospels: one night when the disciples found themselves in a boat on Lake Tiberius and a storm blew up, Jesus came towards them walking on the water. They thought he must be some sort of ghost but Jesus reassured them by saying: "Do not be afraid" (Matthew ch.14, v.27), and he calmed the storm.

2

After two weeks the wind dropped and the monks were exhausted with rowing. In the last rays of the setting sun the tall, upright figure of the old Abbot was silhouetted against the sky as he stood at the prow of the boat. He had no idea which way to steer: all he knew was that he must submit to the divine will, just as his monks submitted to his own authority. With a few words he reassured his crew: "Do not be afraid. God is our pilot. When the wind is right make good use of it; when there is no wind, trust in the Lord."

Jesus walking on the water, from a work by Ghiberti (the Baptistry in Florence, Italy).

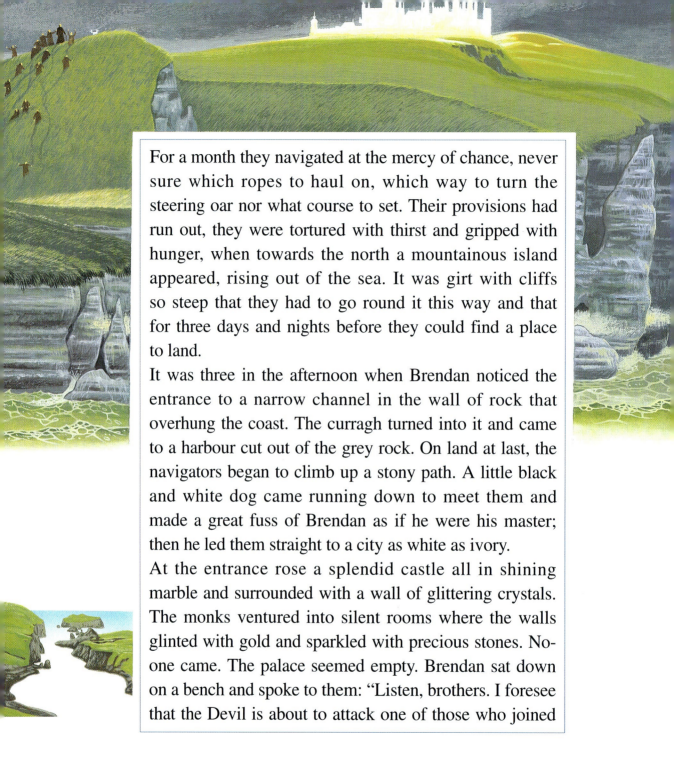

For a month they navigated at the mercy of chance, never sure which ropes to haul on, which way to turn the steering oar nor what course to set. Their provisions had run out, they were tortured with thirst and gripped with hunger, when towards the north a mountainous island appeared, rising out of the sea. It was girt with cliffs so steep that they had to go round it this way and that for three days and nights before they could find a place to land.

It was three in the afternoon when Brendan noticed the entrance to a narrow channel in the wall of rock that overhung the coast. The curragh turned into it and came to a harbour cut out of the grey rock. On land at last, the navigators began to climb up a stony path. A little black and white dog came running down to meet them and made a great fuss of Brendan as if he were his master; then he led them straight to a city as white as ivory.

At the entrance rose a splendid castle all in shining marble and surrounded with a wall of glittering crystals. The monks ventured into silent rooms where the walls glinted with gold and sparkled with precious stones. No-one came. The palace seemed empty. Brendan sat down on a bench and spoke to them: "Listen, brothers. I foresee that the Devil is about to attack one of those who joined

They come ashore on an island.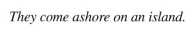

us late at the last minute. Pray for him and go and see if you can find anything for us to eat."

As by a miracle they found plenty of delicious food and cool drink to refresh them. A sumptuous table awaited them decked with beautiful gold and silver dishes. After the meal and the evening prayer the tired monks slept peacefully in beds which seemed to have been carefully prepared for each of them.

But Brendan did not sleep. Although it was very dark, he could make out a devil in the shape of a little black boy who was making a noise with one of the late-comers, laughing and giving him a gold goblet which the monk hid in his clothes. After they had spent three days recovering their strength in this great deserted palace, the monks went back to the harbour. Before setting off again, the Abbot said to them with tears in his eyes: "I beg you, do not take anything from here except the things you brought with you, not a single crumb. Are you sure that there is no thief amongst you?"

Feeling guilty, the monk who had let himself be tempted by the demon took the goblet out of his pocket and fell

The Irish in the Middle Ages knew very little about Africans. The imagery representing demons as black and angels as white had come to them from the writings of the first monks who lived in the 4th century in Egypt, and who shared the racist ideas of their time from encounters with Ethiopians.

Devil comes from the Greek word diabolos, which means one who speaks ill (Satan in Hebrew). In the Middle Ages the Devil was a very important idea, for all evil was believed to come from him.

The Devil works his evil magic.

on his knees before Brendan and implored his pardon before them all.

Brendan simply said: "Pray for his soul, for he will die this very day!" Immediately, shaking with rage, the Devil came out of the body of the one he had possessed and let out a great roar: "Why are you driving me out of my own home, Brendan?" he cried, as he vanished in smoke. After receiving the last sacrament from Brendan's hands, the late-comer gave up the ghost and flew to Paradise, borne up by shining angels, while his companions buried his body on the shore.

Suddenly there appeared before the monks a young messenger, radiant with light, carrying a basket full of loaves of bread and a pitcher of fresh water: "Accept this gift from Heaven," he said to them. "Whatever dangers await you on your voyage, do not be afraid. As for provisions, you need not fear that you will run out of food. These things will be enough for you until you find more elsewhere."

He said no more, simply bowed by way of goodbye. Straightway the navigators returned to the shore; a biting wind filled the sails and drove the boat fast out into the ocean.

A person possessed is a person whom a demon has entered. Exorcism, using prayers to drive out the demon, was common in those days.

Below is a picture of an Irish boat scratched on a cross of the 8th century.

The last sacrament, or communion, involves eating bread and wine blessed by a priest during Mass. For Christians, this represents the body and blood of Christ. From the Middle Ages it became the custom to give communion to a dying person.

Angels accomplish divine missions such as bringing the souls of the just to Paradise. Above is the Prophet Isaiah talking with an angel, from an illuminated manuscript in Reichenau (10th century).

The wind carries the curragh to a land of enormous sheep.

3

Holy Thursday comes before Easter Sunday. It is the Feast commemorating the last meal that Christ shared with his disciples, as told in the Gospels.

For the best part of a year Brendan and his companions ploughed their way through the unexplored ocean. To make their provisions last they ate a meal just once every two days. At last a favourable wind pushed their curragh to a land where they disembarked. Everywhere they saw sheep as big as stags grazing, their fleece a brilliant white. With a fatherly smile, the Abbot said to his monks: "My good friends, today is Holy Thursday. We'll stay here three days. Slaughter a lamb for Easter Day. Let us ask God's permission since there doesn't

They celebrate Easter on an island that turns out to be – a whale!

seem to be anyone here to ask."

The next day a man came whose white hair spoke of age but whose eyes sparkled with youth. He brought them white bread that had been baked in embers, and asked them what else they needed. Brendan tried to question him about how he lived but the man was clearly not inclined to talk. "We lack for nothing, thank you," said Brendan, "we have plenty of all one could wish for."

But he did ask about the amazing size of the sheep. "It's not really surprising," the man explained. "There is no shepherd looking after them. No-one milks the ewes. The air is pure, the winter is not extreme and the sheep never die of disease. Now, Brendan," he went on, "it's time you went back on board. Steer your people to that island you can see over there. You will arrive tonight, and tomorrow you'll celebrate Easter there. Actually you will find yourselves leaving sooner than you intended – you'll soon see why. Then you will go on to another land further west, where I'll join you again, bringing you all that you need."

In the Bible the lamb is the symbol of God's people. When creatures are offered for sacrifice, the lamb is most often chosen. At Jewish Passover a lamb bone is placed on the dish as a reminder of the lambs offered at the Temple in Jerusalem. The lamb is also the symbol of Jesus Christ, who, Christians believe, offered himself to die on the Cross and who was resurrected on Easter Day.

They raised the sail and steered towards the island the messenger had indicated. The boat ran aground before reaching land. Brendan ordered his brothers into the water to haul her up to the shore. There was no beach; the island seemed rocky and devoid of vegetation. They spent the night of Easter eve chanting the sacred office under the starry vault of the heavens. In the morning, after celebrating Mass, the brothers brought ashore the joints of lamb they had cut up three days before; they made a fire and set a cauldron to boil the meat for the Easter meal. The Abbot remained on board for he alone was aware of the sort of island they were dealing with, but he did not tell them because he did not want to frighten them. Suddenly the island started to move and headed away from the boat at great speed. The monks tumbled off and were left struggling in the sea.

"Ahoy there, wait for us..." they yelled to Brendan. They were terrified. He threw ropes to them and they all managed to swim to the boat and climb aboard. The island was already far away but they could still make out the fire they had lit. Brendan told them: "Brothers, do you know what gave you such a fright? You were on the biggest animal that lives in the sea. It's called Jasconius and ever since the world began it has been trying to bite

An office is a service of worship of a religious community. It consists of prayers, chants and ritual gestures.

Ropes have many uses on board ship!

Jasconius comes from the Irish word iasc meaning fish. In the earliest times and in the Middle Ages the ocean was commonly thought to be inhabited by sea monsters, as shown in this English miniature of the 13th century.

its own tail without succeeding!"

The curragh sped over the crests of the waves and soon, as the sun was sinking, a line of land showed white on the horizon. Fearlessly the navigators steered close to the coast and went slowly along a watercourse. This had its source between the roots of a tree of wonderful proportions: its trunk was thick and as white as marble; its wide leaves had purple and silver markings. It towered out of sight among the clouds. A multitude of birds of brilliant plumage made its branches noisy with their chirping; Brendan was intrigued with their charming song. One came and fluttered around the holy man. The beating of its wings made a very soft sound like the tinkling of a bell.

"If you are a creature of God," said the Abbot, "tell me who you are and what brings you to this place; you and your companions all seem so lovely."

The beautiful bird settled on Brendan's right shoulder and fluted in his ear: "We are angels who used to live in Heaven.

The serpent (or animal) biting its tail symbolises infinity, time eternally renewed, something beyond the grasp of this sea monster. Above, the serpent Uroboros, from a 15th-century manuscript.

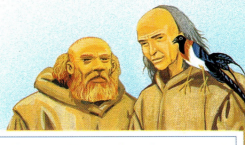

Lucifer, Latin for light-carrier, is a name given – unfairly – to Satan since the Middle Ages. It was the name of the planet Venus, the Morning Star, which sets at the same time as the sun.

The fall of the rebel angels, after a painting on wood of the 14th century.

The true Rising Sun refers to Christ, also known as the Light of the World.

"From such lofty realms we have fallen so low because of one wretch who was too proud. We were vassals of Lucifer, the wisest and most beautiful of God's angels. But he rebelled against the Lord. We remained faithful to the homage we had paid to him. That is why we were not thrown into Hell with those who took the Devil's part. But because we stayed neutral our punishment is to be deprived of the splendour of God enjoyed by those angels who stand close to him at his side. In short, this place is the Paradise of birds."

With these words he flew off to the top of the tree. It would soon be evening; already the light was dying; the various birds' songs became one song in unison giving thanks to God for the visit of the monks. Meanwhile the brothers went and sat beside the river to refresh themselves, and first one then another nodded off and fell soundly asleep.

As soon as dawn lit the sea and the hill, Brendan woke his companions so that they could sing the praises of the true Rising Sun present in their midst, and the chorus of birds took up the refrain in harmony.

They spent two months in that marvellous place: they needed rest themselves and the curragh was in need of repair after nearly a year of sailing. The monks adjusted

In paying homage to his lord, a vassal put himself under the lord's protection and swore an oath of fealty. (Below, a 13th-century seal.)

The Paradise of Birds gives them a welcome respite.

the ties which join the ribs of the boat to the outside of the hull and replaced any leather rotted by salt with patches made from spare hides carefully stitched. The faithful messenger who had sent them so far came back to see them twice a week and brought them food and drink, as much as they wanted. Seven days on from Pentecost they were ready to take to sea again. While the navigators resumed their voyage, the bird, which had been talking to Brendan, came and perched on the top of the mast and sang to them in a human voice: "Brothers, don't be afraid in the difficulties you will be faced with. Paradise is worth it: you have six years still of voyaging before you reach that place and every year you will come back here to celebrate Easter on the whale."

While the birds sang their farewell, the wind filled the sails and the boat sped towards the open sea.

A 15th-century illustration of the *Voyage of Saint Brendan* shows him and his companions on the whale, Jasconius.

Their voyage continues. They are running out of food when they see land.

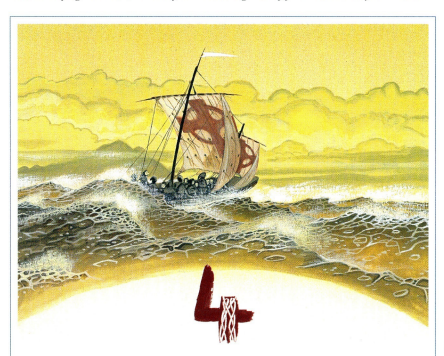

For nearly six months Brendan and his crew sailed on. They were coming to the end of their stores. When finally they sighted land it was impossible to reach it because contrary winds drove them away. For forty days they tried to reach a haven. When they at last succeeded in disembarking, the monks, parched with thirst, made for two springs not far from the shore, one with very clear water, the other clouded. But their Abbot told them: "Wait, brothers. Don't drink from this one. We don't know if it is good."

Saint Brendan and his friends arriving on the Isle of Ailbe (from a 15th-century manuscript).

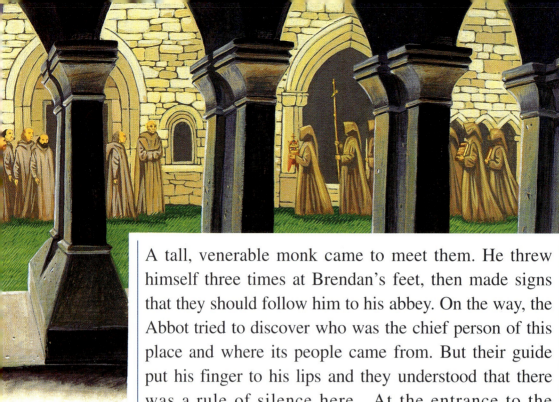

A tall, venerable monk came to meet them. He threw himself three times at Brendan's feet, then made signs that they should follow him to his abbey. On the way, the Abbot tried to discover who was the chief person of this place and where its people came from. But their guide put his finger to his lips and they understood that there was a rule of silence here. At the entrance to the monastery, the most magnificent they had ever seen, eleven brothers came to meet them in procession led by their Abbot, dressed in their ceremonial robes and carrying golden crosses, precious reliquaries and holy books in rich bindings. They gave the exhausted monks the kiss of peace, then took them into the cloisters where they bathed their feet in token of welcome. Afterwards they went on to the refectory to a meal eaten in silence: before each man lay a piece of white bread, a dish of fresh vegetables and a pitcher of water so good it was better than sweet wine. On a sign from the Abbot of this place all rose from the table and made their way to the chapel to give thanks to God. They passed twelve other

Monastic rule (that of Saint Benedict was generally imposed during the Middle Ages) required that monks should not speak when they had nothing to say and should observe silence in church, in the dormitory, and in the kitchen and refectory. The monks perfected a sign language that was still in use until the middle of the 20th century.

The twelve monks are a reminder of the number of apostles Christ chose to be his disciples.

The cloisters were the covered walkways surrounding the inner courtyard to which only monks had access.

A monastic community invites them to celebrate Christmas there.

A reliquary is a precious casket containing the remains (relics) of a saint, revered by the faithful. The reliquary below is Saint Columba's.

A chapel is for private worship (here reserved for monks) as distinct from a parish church which is open to all.

Epiphany is the feast commemorating the three Magi coming to see the infant Jesus. They followed a star that had appeared in the sky to lead them. (Epiphaneia, in Greek, means apparition.)

brothers coming from it to take their turn in the refectory. After they had all chanted the evening prayers their host broke the silence and spoke: "There are twenty-four of us living on this island. A long time ago an angel guided Saint Ailbe here. We joined him and he taught us to obey the rule, as you see, and live in peace. We communicate by signs alone. We do not know where the food comes from that we find set before us each day. From the two springs that you saw one provides the clear water we gave you, the other is hot and is used for washing. Our lamps light up and go out of their own accord at the right time. All we do is give praise to God."

"I have never known a more pleasant place," replied Brendan. "What a joy it would be for my companions and me if you allowed us to stay here with you: we would feel as if we were on the threshold of Paradise."

"Stay and celebrate the feasts of Christmas and Epiphany with us," said the monk. "Then you will have to resume your voyage in quest of the marvels awaiting you."

In due time they set to sea again and by Holy Thursday their boat brought them again to the Island of Sheep. In the harbour the same white-haired messenger awaited them. He had set up a tent for them with a bath and a change of clothes. Brendan washed the feet of his monks,

On the eve of his death, Christ brought his disciples together to celebrate the Jewish Passover. In the course of the evening meal (cena in Latin) he washed their feet, a customary rite of hospitality, as an example to them of humility and brotherly love. Then he gave them bread and wine. Christians share bread and wine each time they take communion. For them these sacred foods symbolise Christ's body and blood.

On the right, celebrating Easter on the whale, from a 17th-century print.

...as the Lord had washed the feet of his apostles and they celebrated the Last Supper in memory of the last meal of Christ. On Holy Saturday they made for the whale that was waiting for them.

"All ashore!" ordered Brendan. Jasconius had kept the cauldron for them that they had left behind on his back the year before! This was reassuring: this time they spent Easter Eve in prayer without fear and celebrated Mass on Easter Sunday. Then they took stores aboard and set sail for the Paradise of Birds.

From a distance they saw the white tree with its sparkling leaves and soon they could make out the birds fluttering in its branches. Over the water came the echo of the melody the birds had sung before to welcome them. The messenger greeted them with a boat full of provisions. "Stay here until the Sunday after Pentecost," he said. "I have to go away, but don't be afraid, I'll be back to help you when you want me."

The pilgrims moored their curragh with strong chains. They spent eight weeks undisturbed on this marvellous island. When it was time to depart a beautiful bird came down to them, flying in a wide circle before alighting on the yard of the boat as if to

Holy Saturday is the day before Easter Sunday.

Pentecost (or Whitsun), is the fiftieth day after Easter, when the Holy Spirit came down among the disciples. It marks the birth of the Church.

At Easter, Jasconius is waiting for them.

The yard is a long pole across the front of the mast that holds up the sail.

Legends from many countries deal in dragons, snake-like monsters. In Ireland there are no snakes. Saint Patrick, the island's patron saint, is said to have driven them out by a miracle. Here the monsters are sea creatures who appear in many tales of wonder. The first mention of the Loch Ness monster in Scotland was told thirteen centuries ago in a *Life of Saint Columba*, an Irish monk.

speak to them. Brendan waved for silence: "Lords," said the bird, "you will come back here every year for the next five years. At Christmas you will go to the Isle of Ailbe. You will commemorate the washing of feet and the Last Supper wherever your host ordains. Easter you will spend on the whale." Thereupon the bird flew up to the top of the tree and the boat sailed out to the ocean. Presently the messenger joined the sailors with a boat loaded with provisions which they took on board. For six weeks a favourable wind carried them westwards. Then the sea became still. And suddenly a storm arose and the whole boat, driven by gale force winds, creaked and groaned. Imagine their horror when they saw racing towards them a monstrous sea serpent with flames gushing from its jaws and a roar like fifteen bulls. Their blood froze in their veins. But Brendan cried: "Don't be afraid! He who trusts his Creator should not fear one of his creatures!"

The serpent was just about to reach the boat when another monster broke surface with a bellow of rage. The first turned against this enemy and the two gigantic beasts reared up to attack each other. Flames from their

nostrils spurted up to the clouds. Their fins clashed like shields and their fangs pierced like swords. Blood poured from their wounds, turning the sea bright red. The second monster was victorious and destroyed the vanquished by biting it clean through into three chunks, and then it disappeared beneath the waves.

The next morning the travellers sighted land. They steered their curragh to shore where they set up their tent in a meadow of flowers. But on the ocean a tempest arose more fiercely than ever. A constant onshore wind made it impossible for them to set to sea again and soon their stores ran out.

However the monks had seen so much already and

Brendan had so often told them to trust in the Lord that they were not too discouraged. In fact, a slice of the dismembered serpent was washed up on the beach on a bed of brown seaweed. "There, my brothers," said the Abbot, "our former enemy has come to our rescue. We have enough to eat for a long time, however loathsome it may seem. Cut it up and preserve the pieces in salt to last us three months."

As soon as the wind changed they set sail again. Every year they came back to the Isle of Ailbe for Christmas. They celebrated Holy Thursday with the messenger who fed them, Easter on Jasconius's back, then on to the Island of Birds for Pentecost.

Suddenly, a strong current sweeps them into the mouth of Hell.

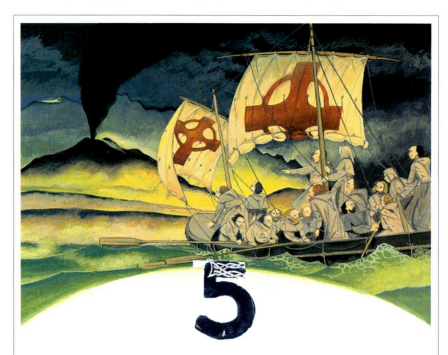

5

As the monks sailed on, the wind drove them northwards. Under grey skies, a jagged outline of land, wrapped in black clouds and gloomy fog, began to appear above the horizon. A smell of sulphur and carrion assailed them. They rowed with all their strength to escape from this terrifying island, but strong currents carried them on. The Abbot felt their anxiety and said to them as he made the sign of the cross: "I must tell you that we are approaching the pit of Hell. You have never been more in need of God's help."

The Irish also tell of a blacksmith god called Goibniu. Here he becomes a devil, but in other Christian accounts he is presented as Goban Saor, a skilled and kindly craftsman. In many ancient religions the blacksmith is given magical powers since he is the master of fire with which powerful weapons are made.

When they came near, live coals rained down around them and blocks of rock split by the fierce heat fell sizzling into the sea. As they were pulled against their will towards an erupting mountain, the monks saw emerge from this Hell a gigantic devil spitting fire and brandishing a huge hammer. As soon as he saw them, the demon blacksmith vanished at once into the smoking pit from whence he had come. Brendan cried to his companions: "Courage, brothers. Grab your oars and row with all your strength. We have to get away from this infernal island. That devil will come back and do his utmost to smash us all to bits." The monster came out again almost at once from his forge holding an enormous piece of red-hot iron in his tongs and with a mighty throw hurled it at them. The great glowing block whistled over their heads scattering sparks and fell into the sea close to the boat.

This demon brings Hephaestus to mind (Vulcan for the Romans), god of Fire and Metallurgy in Greco-Roman mythology. He is described as ugly and deformed. (Below, he is depicted in a Greek ceramic of the 6th century BC.)

"Quick, raise the sail!" Brendan ordered. Providentially, a wind blew them out of reach of the flying brands falling around them. They kept looking back in wonder at the mountain still spitting stinking smoke. Thousands of grinning devils were stamping about on the slopes of the volcanoes; the cries and lamentations of the damned could be distinctly heard. This was all too much for one of the monks – one who had joined the crew at the last minute – he rushed to the prow of the boat and leapt into the sea. Only Brendan saw him jump and saw hundreds of devils come flocking to snatch him away. His former companions noticed nothing but they heard his howl of pain: "It's all my own fault, wretch that I am: my sins are dragging me to the abyss!"

The terrified monks gazed at one another without a word. The clouds parted revealing the mountain and the yawning jaws of its crater: fire and flames were still spouting from it, great balks of blazing timber and white-hot iron, pitch and sulphur shot into the air and fell back into the pit of Hell.

Devil devouring the damned, detail of the *Last Judgement* painted on the dome of the Baptistry in Florence, Italy.

Pitch is a natural bitumen that is highly flammable.

Once more the voyagers find Jasconius and the Isle of Birds.

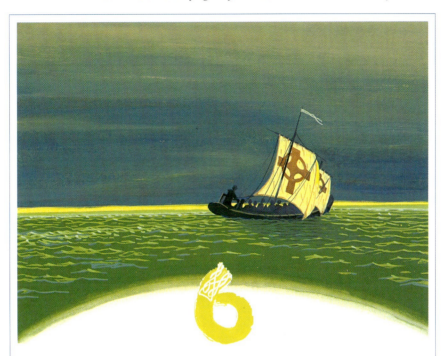

The sea was calm again. With a full spread of sail the monks swiftly distanced themselves from that sinister place. Brendan did a roll call of the crew. One man was found to be missing – the last of the three who had joined the crew late. Only the Abbot knew where he had gone: "God is dealing with him as he sees fit. Let us continue on our way with patience to the Isle of Birds."

This time the faithful, white-haired messenger who had kept them regularly provided came aboard with them. "I have to be your pilot because without me you would

After three days...

never be able to reach your destination." Their course was eastwards. For forty days everything went well: there was only the gentle lapping of waves on the sides of the curragh as it went its way on a sea as smooth as oil. Presently a slight mist formed on the water and began to thicken. As the fog around the boat became ever more dense, their pilot spoke in the darkness to reassure them: "Don't be afraid! This darkness is here to prevent human beings from reaching the Paradise from which Adam, the first human being, was driven." As they approached, the fog split open. Now for three days they advanced quickly along a narrow corridor between thick, black walls of cloud. Then, at long last, they left the clouds behind and found themselves in sight of Paradise. Dazzled, the pilgrims screwed up their eyes: a wall of light brighter than the sun stretched to Heaven and in it were set precious stones that sparkled with a thousand fires: emeralds, sapphires, rubies, beryl,

These three days travelling through darkness call to mind the Gospel account where the same period of time separates the death of Christ from his resurrection.

Beryl is a precious stone that comes in various colours (an emerald, for example is a green beryl). Jews and Christians have given a religious meaning to it. In the Middle Ages it was used to foretell the future.

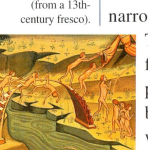

The way leading to Paradise is often preceded by some last ordeal such as a narrow bridge to cross, as depicted below (from a 13th-century fresco).

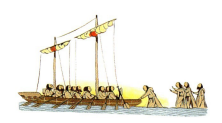

30

...of deepest gloom, Paradise comes into view as a wall of light.

chrysoliths and many other gems shining in all the colours of the rainbow. The sea lapped at the feet of white marble mountains and mountains of pure gold upon which the domain stood. Their pilot guided the curragh straight to the entrance. But two fiery dragons stood on either side of the gate. Above it a sword hung by its hilt, the point in constant swift movement, turning. Anyone trying to force an entry would be pierced by this sword. As soon as the monks set foot ashore, their guide spoke a word and the dragons lay down on the ground; then he raised his hand and put the sword aside. Brendan and his monks followed him into the Garden of Eden. Slowly they advanced over a carpet of white heather.

The way into Paradise is also shown as a ladder with thirty rungs, each of which symbolises a virtue needed by those who aspire to eternal bliss. Above, the Holy Ladder, from a miniature of the 11th-12th century, decorating a text written in the 7th century in a monastery in Sinai (Egypt).

According to the Bible, God planted this paradise Garden "in the East" for Adam and Eve, the first human couple. Tempted by the devil, Adam and Eve disobeyed God and were driven out of Paradise.

They were lost in wonder at the vast prairies covered in flowers, whose sweet scents mingled and perfumed the air. They stood fascinated by butterflies of every hue fluttering from flower to flower making melodious music. No breath of air disturbed the green branches of trees loaded with juicy fruits. Birds of magnificent plumage perched in the branches and raised their voices to heaven in ravishing song. All sorts of animals frolicked in the grass. Fishes with shining scales swam in rivers of milk and honey. On the beds of clear streams lay precious stones. No mountain but it was of gold, no gravel path but it was of silver. The monks were so absorbed in this vision of eternal bliss that they were not aware of time passing.

The messenger took Brendan aside and led him to the top of a grassy hill the height of a cypress tree.

The sight he revealed was quite indescribable: angels celebrated their coming, softly beating their wings and

With this glorious vision in their hearts, they set their course for Ireland.

In the Middle Ages Paradise was imagined as a radiant place where all the senses were overwhelmed with unspeakable happiness. "All this pleasure is a wild wilderness, one finds there neither custom nor road nor retreat, no measure, no end and no beginning, nothing that can be expressed in words." Ruysbroek, 14th century.

Saint Brendan's feast day is May 16th.

singing to the accompaniment of strange instruments. Gently the Abbot's guide took him by the arm: "Further on there are a hundred thousand more glorious sights than you have seen up till now. But for the time being, that is enough for you to bear. Soon you will come back in spirit to where you have been in body and flesh and you will taste completely then these everlasting joys with the myriads of saints who arrived before you. My mission is almost done: I am going to remain here whence I was sent to help you. Take these golden pebbles to give you courage in remembrance."

So saying he brought them back to the gate. Ruefully they unfurled the sail. Joyful winds carried their boat dancing over the waves. In less than three months they reached the green shores of Ireland. All the monks at the monastery which Brendan and his crew had left seven years before rejoiced to see their Abbot again. As for Brendan himself, he would never tire of recounting his adventures to his disciples till the day he died. A radiant smile always lit his face when he tried to describe the marvels of Paradise. And that is where he went one fine May morning... and where we shall meet him again perhaps!

This Irish cross made of granite dates from the 8th century. It is one of the oldest found in Ireland, where there were many throughout the country in the Middle Ages.

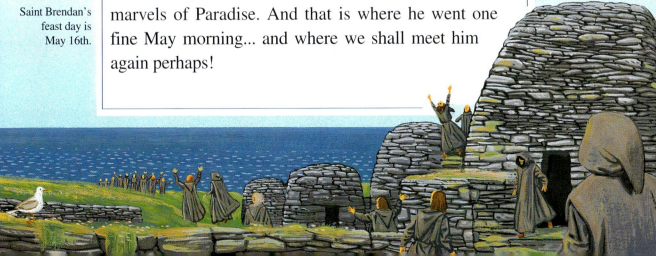

In the 12th century, Normandy, and later much of the west of France as we know it, was part of England, and the English nobility spoke French. *Saint Brendan's Voyage*, by Benedeit, is one of the first accounts written in French.

Who was Saint Brendan?

Brendan lived in Ireland in the 6th century. He was thought to have been born about 490 and died in 577 or 583. He belonged to a branch of the Ciarraige (black people, in Irish), a clan of the west coast, whose name came down to us as Kerry.

A bestseller of the 12th century

Brendan is said to have visited the abbot Columba when in 563 he had retired to Iona, an island off the coast of Scotland. It is possible too that Brendan had travelled the coasts of Britain and Brittany. Such was his reputation as a navigator that his name has been linked with many other adventures. His legendary voyages have been told several times in Latin, perhaps even as early as the end of the 8th century. These were followed by versions in most European languages. Nearly eighty versions have been preserved.

About 1121 a Norman poet, Benedeit, put the text into French verse and made it one of the most popular stories from the Middle Ages. *Saint Brendan's Voyage* could be said to be the epic of the Irish monks in their heyday in the Early Middle Ages.

Did Brendan discover America?

If one tries to find what might be true behind the fantastic incidents told in the *Voyage*, the Isle of Sheep could be one of the Faeroe Islands (the name means sheep in Danish); the hellish islands spitting flames are like Iceland with its volcanoes. Did Brendan reach the Canary Islands, Cuba or America? In the 16th century his paradise still featured on maps. In 1519 a treaty between Spain and Portugal ceded all rights to this island to Spain – should it ever be rediscovered! In 1976 an Irishman, Tim Severin, copied Brendan's curragh and repeated his journey, crossing the Atlantic in two stages.

Left, The Monk Navigator, from a manuscript of the Middle Ages.

The statue of Saint Brendan (above) in the porch of the church in Clonfert.

In the 6th century Saint Kevin founded the monastery of Glendalough (below). The tower served as bell tower and refuge against attacks. The church dates from the 11th century.

For a long time Brendan's Isle was shown on maps in mid-Atlantic. Between 1526 and 1721 four expeditions from the Canaries tried to reach it, without success. They thought at the time that it must be a floating island that took off when explorers came.

How Ireland became Christian

Right, silver interior of a cauldron of the 1st century BC, with Cernunnos, the Celtic god of fertility and the wild forces of Nature. The boar is associated with the spiritual world. The stag stands for riches and fecundity.

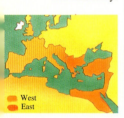

The Roman Empire in the middle of the 5th century.

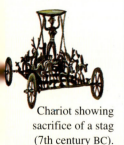

Chariot showing sacrifice of a stag (7th century BC).

In Celtic mythology, the oak tree is the visible form of the divinity. Mistletoe, a plant from the other world, heals all ills.

Christianity was imposed throughout the Roman Empire. Ireland, which had never been colonised by Rome, kept its traditional beliefs, that is, the Celtic religion, until the 5th century.

The Celtic religion

The supreme god was Lug; Dagda, the good god, like the god of the Gauls, Taranis, was lord of the Elements, Science and Eternity. His daughter was Bridget, the only female god, who would later be confused with a saint. Under the name of Boand – the river Boyne – she was the wife of her paternal uncle, Elcmar the Jealous, also known as Ogme. It was he, a magician and warrior, who invented writing. The Celts believed in the soul's immortality. Those who died went to another world, the Sid.

Druids, prophets and bards

These were the sacred classes. Druids (the word means very learned) were the keepers of knowledge. They presided over rituals and ceremonies. They assured morals and enjoyed high esteem. They passed on knowledge but only by word of mouth, leaving no written texts. This elite class soon became troublesome to Christianity spreading from Rome which finally banned druidism.

Prophets were priests; they performed rituals and sacrifices and practised medical arts as well as divination.

In the Middle Ages Ireland was made up of five regions which still exist today: Ulster, Munster, Leinster, Connaught and Meath (from the Irish Mide, meaning the Centre).

Celtic crosier set with precious stones (12th century).

Left, one of the first Irish representations of the Crucifixion, which would serve as a model for a long time (decorated bronze plaque from the early 8th century)

Saint Patrick, Druid of God

During the 5th century Ireland was gradually converted to Christianity by missionaries from Britain. The most famous was Saint Patrick; he died in about 492. When he was sixteen he was captured by Irish pirates and sold as a slave in their island. It is said that he managed to escape some years later and returned to Britain, or to Gaul, where he completed his religious education. Then he asked the British bishops to send him to Ireland to teach the Gospels.

Saint Patrick's fame has tended to eclipse other missionaries, such as Saint Ailbe, who may have converted the south-west of Ireland (Munster) and who died in about 527.

Colomba, who died in 597, was possibly heir to the most powerful royal line of kings, and was a monk and abbot with numerous monasteries, thus he may have been seen as having too much power concentrated in him. Doubtless that was why he had to consent to exile himself to the Scottish island of Iona in 563.

For several generations Christianity and traditional beliefs coexisted in people's practices and in their minds. Individuals saw nothing odd about practising both religions. So Christianity came in gradually and almost without conflict.

Travelling monks

From the 6th century the particular characteristics of Irish Christianity become clear: its vitality, its power to expand and its fondness for travel. Monks went to continental Europe where they played an important role. Colomba travelled through Gaul, and founded the monastery of Luxeuil in the Vosges, about 590, and another at Bobbio in Italy, where he died.

Monasticism developed very rapidly. Many monasteries became great learning centres (Armagh, Iona, Kells...). As early as the 7th century documents mention monks who may have taken to the sea in search of uninhabited islands. It was Irish hermits who, during the 7th and 8th centuries, settled in islands to the north of Scotland (the Faeroes, the Hebrides) and even in Iceland, in about 795.

Bards sang the praises of warriors or satirised them.

Recent statue of Saint Colomba. Luxeuil, France.

Centre, top of page Saint Patrick

Following the example of Saint Anthony – considered as the father of Christian monks – who, in about 270, retired to the Egyptian desert, many were attracted to the hermit's life. Irish monks sought retreat on islands.

Casket of bronze and silver for Saint Patrick's bell (10th-11th century)

An 8th-century chalice, a masterpiece of Irish religious art. In Ireland chalices were made of wood, glass, bronze, perhaps even of stone.

In Brendan's time Gaul was divided between the descendants of Clovis. It would be many centuries before it became France.

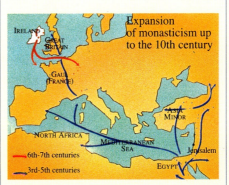

Expansion of monasticism up to the 10th century

Monastic life

The monastery of Kells, founded by Saint Columba.

Until the 15th century books were made of parchment. Monks copied the ancient texts.

Skins were scraped, rubbed smooth, cut up.

Tools used by the monk copyist.

An illuminated manuscript had decorated letters and miniature illustrations.

Irish and Breton monks went about with a staff like a crook and a bell (to drive away demons) as shown in the 8th century sculpture at the top of the page. The front of the head was shaved and the hair left long at the back. They carried a bag on their shoulders containing a prayer book which they read continually.

Ornamented letter from an Irish Gospel, *The Book of Kells* (about 800), a superb example of Celtic illumination.

Under the abbot's authority

Monks lived communally, and they followed a Rule – a sort of guide to community living to help each man pursue his spiritual vocation. In Brendan's time each monastery worked out its own rule, often placing itself under the abbot's authority. He was the father and master of the monks. In Ireland the abbot was generally the heir of the founder and frequently of royal lineage. In the 12th century, when Benedeit adapted the old medieval legend of Saint Brendan to suit the tastes of the nobility of his own time, the Rule of Benedict was accepted throughout Europe and no-one imagined that Brendan and his monks could have lived differently.

The Rule, instituted by Saint Benedict in Southern Italy in the middle of the 6th century, divided the monks' day between manual work, spiritual reading and communal prayer. The monks' vocation was to maintain constant service to God – praising and glorifying God at regular hours both day and night.

An Irish monk's day

Thanks to the monastic Rules drawn up at the end of the 6th century by Saint Colomba, it is possible to show how Celtic monks passed their days between eight religious services and work:

Midnight Wake and sing the service (later known as *Compline*). Second sleep.
About 4 am Grand Vigil (or *Matins*): Sing 24-36 psalms from the Bible. Time for washing.
About 6 am Teaching by the abbot, followed on Sundays and religious feast days by Mass.
About 7 am *Secunda*. Service of the second hour. End of the night's silence.
About 8 am *Terce*. Service of the third hour, then manual labour, tending crops, copying manuscripts.
Midday *Sext*. Service of the sixth hour. Work.
About 2 pm *None*. Service of the ninth hour. Reading, confession, penance.
About 4 pm Vegetarian meal.
About 5pm *Duodecima*. Service of the twelfth hour. Liturgy of peace (for brothers who died in their sleep). Bed.

In the 6th century hours did not have sixty minutes; they varied with the seasons: one hour was the twelfth part of the day or night.

In quest of Paradise

Top: crossing the Styx, the river leading to the Underworld in Greek mythology (after J. Patinir, 16th century).

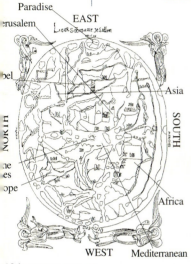

12th-century map

The tale of Brendan's voyage, in the context of the monastic day's rhythm, and recurring feast days, can be read as a meditation on the quest for salvation.

Greek and Roman mythology placed early humanity in a lush garden from which suffering was excluded. Poets of antiquity described a lost golden age which the just would rediscover after death. In the biblical tradition it is Paradise; for the ancient Greeks and Romans it was The Elysian Fields. In *The Odyssey* the Greek poet Homer (9th-8th century BC) spoke of a place "right at the end of the earth", towards the west: life there was sweet, the weather always mild. The Latin poet Virgil, writing 30 years before Christ, put it at the heart of the Underworld. In his long poem, the *Aeneid*, he described it as an enchanting land, reserved for the just and for heroes.

Ireland had its own tradition of other world stories told by the druids. From 575, many of these poets, converted to Christianity, became monks and wrote down these tales that had been passed on orally for hundreds of years. Thus were the *echtrai* born (the word means departure, excursion), which tell how the hero, often invited by a supernatural messenger, reached the other world after a short voyage. In those far off, wonderful islands time, distance and pain were unknown. The *immrama* (or act of rowing round) in a christianised form, placed more emphasis on the efforts needed to reach Paradise than on the splendours to be found there. The *Immram of Mael Duin* was a model for *The Voyage of Brendan*: the hero takes to the sea to avenge his murdered father and is carried away in a storm. The tale tells of some thirty islands, all full of wonders, that he comes upon in the course of his voyaging.

A text of the 7th century tells how Bran and his friends ventured as far as the Isle of Women, where they did not notice time passing. On their return to Ireland the first man to land turned to dust as if he had been dead for centuries. They learn that *The Voyage of Bran* is a very old story from ancient times. So Bran returned to the sea and was never seen again.

In *The Divine Comedy*, the poet Dante visits Purgatory before arriving in Paradise (14th century miniature).

39

Look out for other titles in this series:

SARAH, WHO LOVED LAUGHING
A TALE FROM THE BIBLE

THE SECRETS OF KAIDARA
AN ANIMIST TALE FROM AFRICA

I WANT TO TALK TO GOD
A TALE FROM ISLAM

THE RIVER GODDESS
A TALE FROM HINDUISM

CHILDREN OF THE MOON
YANOMAMI LEGENDS

I'LL TELL YOU A STORY
TALES FROM JUDAISM

THE PRINCE WHO BECAME A BEGGAR
A BUDDHIST TALE

JESUS SAT DOWN AND SAID...
THE PARABLES OF JESUS

SAINT FRANCIS, THE MAN WHO SPOKE TO BIRDS
TALES OF ST FRANCIS OF ASSISI

THE MAGIC OF CHRISTMAS
CHRISTMAS TALES FROM EUROPE

MUHAMMAD'S NIGHT JOURNEY
A TALE FROM ISLAM

RAMA, THE HEROIC PRINCE
A HINDU TALE FROM THE RAMAYANA